W9-DFG-832

Jeff
Gordon

Jeff Gordon

By Laurie Collier Hillstrom

LUCENT BOOKS
A part of Gale, Cengage Learning

GALE
CENGAGE Learning

Detroit • New York • San Francisco • New Haven, Conn • Waterville, Maine • London

LIBRARY OF CONGRESS CATALOGING-IN-PUBLICATION DATA

Hillstrom, Laurie Collier, 1965-
  Jeff Gordon / by Laurie Collier Hillstrom.
    p. cm. -- (People in the news)
  Includes bibliographical references and index.
  ISBN 978-1-4205-0606-8 (hardcover)
1. Gordon, Jeff, 1971- 2. Automobile racing drivers--United States--Biography. I. Title.
  GV1032.G67H57 2011
  796.72092--dc22
  [B]
                                                        2011003924

Lucent Books
27500 Drake Rd
Farmington Hills MI 48331

ISBN-13: 978-1-4205-0606-8
ISBN-10: 1-4205-0606-4

Printed in the United States of America
1 2 3 4 5 6 7 15 14 13 12 11

Printed by Bang Printing, Brainerd, MN, 1ˢᵗ Ptg., 06/2011

Contents

F ame and celebrity are alluring. People are drawn to those who walk in fame's spotlight, whether they are known for great accomplishments or for notorious deeds. The lives of the famous pique public interest and attract attention, perhaps because their experiences seem in some ways so different from, yet in other ways so similar to, our own.

Newspapers, magazines, and television regularly capitalize on this fascination with celebrity by running profiles of famous people. For example, television programs such as *Entertainment Tonight* devote all their programming to stories about entertainment and entertainers. Magazines such as *People* fill their pages with stories of the private lives of famous people. Even newspapers, newsmagazines, and television news frequently delve into the lives of well-known personalities. Despite the number of articles and programs, few provide more than a superficial glimpse at their subjects.

Lucent's People in the News series offers young readers a deeper look into the lives of today's newsmakers, the influences that have shaped them, and the impact they have had in their fields of endeavor and on other people's lives. The subjects of the series hail from many disciplines and walks of life. They include authors, musicians, athletes, political leaders, entertainers, entrepreneurs, and others who have made a mark on modern life and who, in many cases, will continue to do so for years to come.

These biographies are more than factual chronicles. Each book emphasizes the contributions, accomplishments, or deeds that have brought fame or notoriety to the individual and shows how that person has influenced modern life. Authors portray their subjects in a realistic, unsentimental light. For example, Bill Gates—the cofounder and chief executive officer of the software giant Microsoft—has been instrumental in making personal computers the most vital tool of the modern age. Few dispute his business savvy, his perseverance, or his technical expertise, yet critics say he is ruthless in his dealings with competitors and driven more by his desire to maintain Microsoft's dominance in the computer industry than by an interest in furthering technology.

In these books, young readers will encounter inspiring stories about real people who achieved success despite enormous obstacles. Oprah Winfrey—the most powerful, most watched, and wealthiest woman on television today—spent the first six years of her life in the care of her grandparents while her unwed mother sought work and a better life elsewhere. Her adolescence was colored by pregnancy at age fourteen, rape, and sexual abuse.

Each author documents and supports his or her work with an array of primary and secondary source quotations taken from diaries, letters, speeches, and interviews. All quotes are footnoted to show readers exactly how and where biographers derive their information and provide guidance for further research. The quotations enliven the text by giving readers eyewitness views of the life and accomplishments of each person covered in the People in the News series.

In addition, each book in the series includes photographs, annotated bibliographies, timelines, and comprehensive indexes. For both the casual reader and the student researcher, the People in the News series offers insight into the lives of today's newsmakers—people who shape the way we live, work, and play in the modern age.

Changing the Face of NASCAR

J eff Gordon is one of the most successful drivers in the history
of NASCAR (National Association for Stock Car Auto Racing).
By 2011, Gordon's career statistics included eighty-two race victories (first among current active drivers), four Winston Cup
championships, and more than $83 million in prize money. He
is widely considered to be NASCAR's most-talented, all-around
driver. Gordon has won every major race, including the prestigious Daytona 500. He has also demonstrated a rare ability to
win races on every type of NASCAR track, from high-banked
superspeedways to twisty road courses.

Gordon exploded onto the NASCAR scene in 1993, and earned
the Winston Cup Rookie of the Year Award. Just two years later,
in 1995, he shocked many race fans by edging out legendary
driver Dale Earnhardt Sr. to win the Winston Cup championship.
At twenty-four years old, Gordon became the youngest driver in
NASCAR history to capture the coveted title.

As Gordon emerged as a dominant force on the track, he also
transformed the public image of stock-car racing. Among its many
hard-core fans, NASCAR had long been viewed as the realm of
rugged Southern "good old boys" who grew up working on cars
and paid their dues by bumping fenders on rural racetracks. To the
dismay of people who wanted to preserve this tradition, Gordon
represented a new and different type of NASCAR champion. He
was young and handsome, presented a clean-cut image, came from
California, and got his start in Midwestern open-wheel racing.

Jeff Gordon's clean-cut image and success is credited with broadening NASCAR's fan base and popularity.

By winning four Winston Cup titles in seven years, Gordon became the face of NASCAR in the late 1990s and early 2000s. He also became one of America's most recognizable athletes. Thanks in part to Gordon's widespread appeal, NASCAR experienced remarkable growth and expanded its popularity nationwide during that time. While Gordon attracted millions of enthusiastic new fans to stock-car racing, however, his tremendous success and rapid rise to stardom also generated some resentment among NASCAR traditionalists. "Depending upon which fan you ask and which finger he's pointing," writer Jeff MacGregor explains in *Sports Illustrated* magazine, Gordon "is either This Nation's Mightiest Hero, the Unyielding Defender of True-Blue Decency and the Blessed Four-Barrel Redeemer of the Pushrod V-8 [Engine]; or the Citified, Sissified, Goody Too-Good-to-Be-True Shoes Destroyer of All That Was Once Holy and Noble in the Manly Art of Stock Car Racing."[1]

Although the 2011 season marks a decade since Gordon captured his fourth cup title in 2001, he remains one of NASCAR's best-known drivers. He also remains highly competitive in the No. 24 DuPont Chevrolet. In fact, Gordon has consistently threatened to win a fifth career championship, finishing second in the point standings in 2007 and third in both 2004 and 2009. Entering the 2011 season with a highly respected new crew chief, Alan Gustafson, Gordon appears well positioned to complete his "drive for five." "I believe that life is a very long race, one with a lot of good runs, and a few bad ones," Gordon says. "The team and I are ready for the next challenge."[2]

Chapter 1

Racing Through Childhood

Jeffrey Michael Gordon was born on August 4, 1971, in Vallejo, California, a middle-class community located about 25 miles (40km) from San Francisco. His biological parents, William Grinnell Gordon and Carol Ann Gordon, divorced when he was less than a year old. Jeff's mother supported him and his older sister, Kimberly, by working at a medical supply company. It was there that she met John Bickford, a divorced engineer who owned a small business that manufactured vehicle controls for people with disabilities. Bickford loved cars and was a huge fan of auto racing. When he and Carol started dating, he often took her and the kids to races at the local Vallejo Speedway. In 1973 the couple married, and Bickford joined the family as Jeff and Kimberly's stepfather.

Gordon shared his stepfather's love of racing from an early age. He was not content just to watch races, though, and soon began competing in them. Gordon always enjoyed going fast on any wheeled contraption he could find, including skateboards, roller skates, and bicycles. He started racing a BMX bicycle on dirt tracks when he was only four years old. Even though he was always the smallest kid entered in the BMX races, he often managed to beat much older boys. "Winning was fun," he recalls, "even for a kid who could barely read the words on the trophies he was getting."[3]

Gordon's BMX-racing career was cut short by his mother, who worried that he was going to hurt himself. "They were hauling

Gordon's stepfather John Bickford, left, posing with Gordon and his mother, Carol. John shared his love of racing with his young stepson and encouraged him to try the sport.

the older kids away in an ambulance with broken arms, broken legs, cracked ribs," she remembers. "So I complained to John, 'Isn't there something we can do that's a little bit safer than this?'"[4] A week later, Bickford brought home a pair of quarter-midget race cars—one for five-year-old Jeff to drive and the other for spare parts. These tiny, open-wheel racing machines consisted of a compartment just big enough for a driver to sit in, a roll cage for safety, four wheels that extended outward from the sides of the car (rather than being covered by fenders), and a one-cylinder, 2.85-horsepower engine. Although Gordon's mother expressed doubt that a quarter-midget race car was safer than a BMX bike, Bickford convinced her that the roll cage would protect Jeff from injury.

Gordon happily gave up BMX racing in favor of quarter-midget racing. He and his stepfather built a dirt track in a nearby field, and Gordon practiced driving every day when Bickford got home from work. Bickford used a stopwatch to time each lap around the track. Then he asked Gordon to try driving through the corners differently to see whether changing his approach made him faster or slower. Jeff's mother also helped prepare him for race conditions by driving around the track in the second car, passing him, and getting in his way. Before long Gordon was ready to enter races near his home in Northern California. By the time he was six years old, he had won thirty-five local races and set several track records. At this point, Gordon and his stepfather began traveling to tracks across the country for races. Despite facing stiffer competition, Gordon kept on winning. In 1979, at the age of eight, he notched fifty-two race victories and claimed his first quarter-midget national championship.

Competes in Go-Karts and Sprint Cars

After winning a second quarter-midget championship in 1981, Gordon transitioned to go-kart racing. Go-karts are slightly larger than quarter midgets but share the same basic design. Powered by 10-horsepower engines, they are faster and more difficult to handle than the smaller cars. Nevertheless, Gordon easily adapted his driving skills to go-karts and continued winning races. At the age of nine, he went undefeated in the twenty-five speedway events he entered in California. Gordon regularly beat drivers in their late teens, and some of his competitors were not pleased about it. "In every car and every league I'd ever raced in, I was always the youngest and the smallest. I experienced a lot of jealousy and resentment at every level," he explains. "I was used to the names—kid, boy, squirt, even a few punks—but I always laughed them off."[5]

When Gordon was thirteen, his stepfather felt that he was ready to move up to the next level of racing: sprint cars. Like quarter midgets and go-karts, sprint cars are small, open-wheel cars designed to race on short, oval-shaped dirt tracks with banked turns. But sprint cars have much more powerful engines and are capable of reaching speeds up to 140 miles per hour (225 kmh). "Imagine a lawn tractor with a 700-horsepower engine shoehorned into it, and you'll have a good idea what a sprint car looks like,

Thirteen-year-old Gordon participates in a sprint car race in 1984 after years of developing his skills racing quarter midgets and go-karts.

and how it handles," writes MacGregor in *Sports Illustrated*. "It is a horrifying, primitive machine, all neck-snapping straight-line acceleration and Ben-Hur [a 1959 film featuring a violent chariot race] terror in the turns."[6]

United States Auto Club

Jeff Gordon spent his early career driving open-wheel cars in races sanctioned by the United States Auto Club (USAC). USAC primarily consists of four race series—Silver Crown, Sprint Car, Midget, and Ford Focus—each of which features a different type of car and track. Silver Crown cars are the largest and compete on tracks greater than 1 mile (1.6km) in length. Midget cars are the smallest and compete on tracks shorter than 0.5 mile (0.8km) in length.

Gordon celebrates a USAC Silver Crown sprint car victory in Phoenix, Arizona, in 1991.

The different USAC series expose drivers to a variety of racing conditions and help them improve their skills. "You learn to be versatile racing in USAC," says Tony Stewart, a four-time USAC champion and two-time NASCAR Nextel Cup champion. "You race a 900-pound Midget, a 1,200-pound Sprint Car, a 1,400-pound Silver Crown Car on dirt and asphalt—three different types of cars on two different surfaces at tracks ranging from half-mile up to mile and a half. Because you have to constantly adjust to each one, it doesn't get you in a habit or pattern."

Gordon won national championships in two USAC series: Midget in 1990 and Silver Crown in 1991. He then became one of the first USAC champions to make the jump to closed-wheel, stock-car racing. When Gordon emerged as a dominant force in NASCAR during the late 1990s, team owners increasingly began combing the ranks of USAC drivers in search of the next superstar. Like Gordon and Stewart, USAC champions Ryan Newman and Kasey Kahne also switched to NASCAR.

Rob Fisher. "Midget Racing—The Many Faces of USAC: From the County Fair to the World's Fair, USAC Has It All." *Circle Track*, February 2009. http://www.circletrack.com/featuredvehicles/ctrp_0702_usac_racing/index.html.

Since Gordon was still too young to get a driver's license, Bickford initially had trouble convincing race organizers and fellow sprint car owners to allow his stepson to compete. Some people even accused Bickford of recklessly endangering the boy to fulfill his own racing fantasies. But Gordon loved racing and was determined to test his driving skills against tougher competition. They eventually found a sprint-car race circuit in Florida that did not have a minimum-age requirement, and in February 1985 Bickford drove Gordon across the country to enter a five-race series. When Gordon arrived in Florida and climbed into the driver's seat of his sprint car—which had to be specially equipped with a booster so he could reach the steering wheel and gas pedal—it was the first time he had ever driven the powerful new machine. Comparing the experience to driving a quarter midget, he said it "was like going from a single-engine Cessna [a small airplane] to an F-16"[7] military fighter jet.

Although it took Gordon some time to get used to the new car, he learned quickly and improved his performance with every outing. Since sprint cars served as a training ground for up-and-coming young racers, Gordon faced stiffer competition than ever before. But he still managed to reach the winner's circle for the first time at a 1986 race in Chillicothe, Ohio. Another highlight of Gordon's early sprint-car career came when he ended up racing against Steve Kinser, a veteran driver who had won multiple championships in the World of Outlaws professional dirt-track series. Gordon led the race for several laps, but Kinser claimed the victory. Afterward, the teenager was thrilled when Kinser stopped by his trailer to praise his driving ability.

Moves to Indiana

By the time Gordon turned fourteen, he had proven that he could dominate the competition near his home in Northern California. He thus spent nearly every weekend and school vacation on the road, traveling throughout the Midwest to compete in sprint-car races. Over time, though, the constant travel between California and the Midwest became increasingly difficult to manage. To continue to challenge himself and develop his driving skills, Gordon

The legendary Indianapolis Motor Speedway was not far from Gordon's new home when the family moved from California to Indiana to support his racing activities.

needed to be closer to the action. His parents made the difficult decision to disrupt their own lives in order to give him that opportunity. They sold Bickford's business and their home in Vallejo and moved across the country to Pittsboro, Indiana. "It was one of those crossroads in life you come to where you're going to have to make a commitment to something, whether it's your life or your kid's life," Bickford explains. "And I felt the potential in our family lay in our ability to do what it took to advance the kid."[8]

Pittsboro is located about 20 miles (32km) from Indianapolis, in the heart of open-wheel racing country. The legendary Indianapolis Motor Speedway in Indiana hosts the annual Indianapolis 500, which is one of the oldest and most prestigious auto races in the world. As a lifelong race fan, Gordon had grown up watching the Indianapolis 500 on television. He considered some of the top drivers—such as four-time winner A.J. Foyt—to be his heroes. When his family moved to Pittsboro, it was a major thrill for him to visit the famous, century-old track, which is known as the Brickyard because of the row of original bricks that remain in place at the start-finish line.

Upon moving to Indiana, Gordon entered Tri-West High School in Lizton. Although his busy race schedule did not leave much time for extracurricular activities, he did find time to play saxophone in the school band. He also joined the Tri-West cross-country team in order to improve his fitness for driving. Throughout his high school years, Gordon's favorite subject was science. Recognizing his strong interest in cars, his teacher encouraged him to do science projects on topics that had automotive applications, such as wind resistance, speed and velocity, and internal combustion engines. Gordon was a popular student, thanks in part to his growing fame as a race-car driver. During his senior year in 1989, his classmates voted him prom king.

Although racing caused Gordon to miss out on some activities enjoyed by other teenagers—like high school dances and football games—he felt that it also presented him with valuable opportunities that were not available to his peers. "One of the questions I'm asked more than any other is if I somehow feel cheated out of a childhood. Not only is the answer absolutely not, I'm always a little surprised by the question," he says. "Before my 18th birthday, I won 600 races, traveled to the other side of the world, drove almost every square mile of this country, met thousands of people, learned about business, economics, marketing, sales, and the value of relationships—all while doing the thing I wanted to do more than eat, drink, or breathe."[9]

Steadily Gains Exposure

The move to Indiana had its intended effect on Gordon's racing career. He competed on tracks throughout the Midwest during his high school years, advancing through the ranks of short-track

In 1989 Gordon began racing midget cars, similar to those in this photo, with the United States Auto Club (USAC), winning Rookie of the Year honors.

racing and making a name for himself as one of the best young drivers in the country. But the move also created some financial hardships for his family. For a while, they lived on the proceeds from the sale of Bickford's business and the prize money Gordon earned by winning races. Their racing effort operated on a very small budget during those years. "We slept in pickup trucks and made our own parts," his stepfather recalls. "That's why I think Jeff is misunderstood by people who think he was born to rich parents."[10]

When he was not racing, Gordon spent a lot of time asking representatives of racing-supply companies for free parts and equipment in exchange for placing a sticker advertising their products on his car. He remembers one occasion when he walked into the Valvoline offices in Indianapolis to try to talk his way into getting a free case of motor oil. Shocked at being approached by a fourteen-year-old, the sales representative asked how he had managed to get there. Gordon replied simply, "My mom drove me. How about that oil?"[11] Gordon's relentless self-promotion eventually paid off. While he was still in high school, Gordon received an offer of sponsorship from John Rae, an Australian racing enthusiast. Since racing can cost thousands of dollars, drivers need a sponsor, like a race-car owner or a corporation, who will pay a certain amount for a car, mechanics, and other expenses. Rae paid some of the young driver's race entry fees and travel expenses, and he also helped out with the cost of car parts and maintenance. His support also made it possible for Gordon to spend a season competing on race circuits in Australia and New Zealand, where he won fourteen out of the fifteen races he entered.

Despite the tight budget, Gordon continued to shine on the track. At sixteen, he became the youngest person ever to earn a competition license from the United States Auto Club (USAC), the main sanctioning organization for open-wheel racing in America. In 1989 he competed in USAC's midget division—which featured 900-pound (408kg) cars powered by 350-horsepower engines racing on tight, 0.5-mile (0.8m) tracks—and earned Rookie of the Year honors. The following year Gordon won nine races in twenty-one starts to claim the USAC midget national championship, becoming the youngest driver ever to do so. He then moved up to USAC's silver crown division, which featured larger, heavier cars racing on longer tracks. He surprised many veterans by winning the 1991 national championship during his first silver crown campaign.

Decides to Join NASCAR

As Gordon accumulated championship trophies in various USAC series, he steadily gained national exposure. He became a fixture on the cable-television sports network ESPN, making regular appearances on its *Speedweek* and *Thursday Night Thunder* programs. Racing insiders predicted that Gordon would soon rate a tryout in the big leagues of professional auto racing. Which circuit he would choose was the subject of much speculation.

Many people believed that Gordon—with his background in open-wheel racing and his roots in Indianapolis—would choose to drive Indy cars in races sanctioned by Championship Auto Racing Teams (CART), including the Indianapolis 500. Indianapolis Motor Speedway owner Tony George thought that Gordon had the potential to increase the popularity of Indy cars and made a determined effort to convince him to join the CART circuit. Other people thought that Gordon's future might lie in Formula One, a glamorous open-wheel racing circuit that holds grand-prix races across Europe.

NASCAR's Origins

Stock-car racing got its unofficial start in the American South during Prohibition, a period when the U.S. government outlawed the sale and distribution of alcohol. Some people flaunted the unpopular law by hiring drivers with fast cars to deliver illegal homemade liquor known as moonshine. After Prohibition ended, former moonshiners often got together on country roads and oval dirt tracks to drive their souped-up cars in races.

By the mid-1940s, a thriving auto-racing culture had developed throughout the region. A driver, mechanic, and race promoter named William "Big Bill" France decided that stock-car racing would benefit from greater organization. In 1948 he and a group of interested drivers and track officials formed the National Association for Stock Car Auto Racing (NASCAR) to serve as a sanctioning body for the sport and ensure that various racing leagues used a consistent set of rules.

NASCAR held its first race the following year in Charlotte, North Carolina. Over the next half century, stock-car racing exploded in popularity. By 2010 NASCAR sanctioned about fifteen hundred events at approximately one hundred tracks across the country each year. The most famous NASCAR race series is the Sprint Cup (formerly known as the Winston Cup and the Nextel Cup).

Cars line up at the start of the first NASCAR race in Charlotte, North Carolina, in June 1949.

Gordon's third option for a professional racing career was in closed-wheel competition sanctioned by the National Association for Stock Car Auto Racing (NASCAR). Unlike open-wheel cars, which are specially built for racing, stock cars are modified, high-performance versions of the mass-production vehicles that are sold to the public in auto dealerships. NASCAR racers are much bigger and heavier than open-wheel racers, with full bodywork and an enclosed cockpit for the driver. Few people thought that Gordon would feel comfortable racing stock cars, since they were so different from anything he had driven before. In addition, the NASCAR circuit was centered in the South and lacked the national visibility and appeal of the open-wheel racing leagues.

Nonetheless, at the suggestion of his stepfather, Gordon decided to give stock cars a try. In 1990 he agreed to attend a driving school run by two-time NASCAR Winston Cup champion Buck Baker at Rockingham Speedway in North Carolina. Baker let Gordon attend for free in exchange for allowing a film crew from ESPN to record his experiences. As it turned out, Gordon absolutely loved driving stock cars. He completed the driving school and was determined to make a career in NASCAR. "After turning a few laps, I was home," he recalls. "I was 19 years old, and I knew what I wanted to do with my career."[12]

Chapter 2

Breaking into NASCAR

Shortly after completing the Buck Baker Driving School, Gordon got his first opportunity to compete in a NASCAR race. He drove a car owned by Hugh Connerty Jr., president of the Outback Steakhouse restaurant chain, in the 1990 AC Delco 200 Busch Grand National Series event at Rockingham Speedway in North Carolina. The Busch Series (later known as the Nationwide Series after it changed sponsors) was the second-highest level of NASCAR racing after the Winston Cup Series (later known as the Nextel Cup Series and the Sprint Cup Series). The two series typically raced at the same track on consecutive days. Busch cars were slightly smaller, lighter, and less powerful than Winston Cup cars, making them more stable and easier to handle. The Busch Series thus served as a proving ground for talented newcomers to gain experience before moving up to Winston Cup. Established Winston Cup drivers sometimes competed in Busch races, too, in order to log practice time on unfamiliar tracks or test out new equipment.

Gordon performed impressively in the prerace qualifying sessions, which are used to determine cars' starting positions for the race. He completed the second-fastest qualifying lap, which allowed him to start his first Busch race in second place (on the outside of the first row). Unfortunately, the race did not go as well. Gordon's day ended early when he crashed on Lap 23. Gordon signed on to drive in two more Busch races for Connerty that season, but he failed to post a fast-enough qualifying time to make the field for either one. Gordon's initial NASCAR experience did

The Pit Crew

Since most NASCAR races are hundreds of miles long, the cars cannot complete an entire race without stopping to refuel and change tires. Pit stops, therefore, are a key component of every race. Drivers who spend less time in the pits are able to gain valuable time and track position on their competitors.

NASCAR rules allow a total of seven crew members per car to go "over the wall" into the pit lane during a race. Each of the seven crew members has a specific job to do. Refueling is handled by the gas-can man, who pours gasoline from a can into the back of the race car, and the catch-can man, who takes away the empty can and provides a replacement. Five other crew members change the tires on the vehicle. They are the front and rear tire carriers, the front and rear tire changers, and the jack man.

A typical NASCAR pit crew can change four tires and refuel a car in about fourteen seconds. If needed, the crew can also make adjustments to the suspension and repair bodywork that has sustained damage on the track. Hendrick Motorsports and other NASCAR teams practice constantly to streamline their pit stops and shave precious seconds off of the time required to refuel and change tires.

Pit crew members scramble to tend to Gordon's No. 24 car and Dale Earnhardt Jr.'s No. 8 car at a stop during a race at Martinsville Speedway in 2004. The speed and precision of a pit crew's work is key to a racer's success.

provide one unexpected benefit, though: As a member of Connerty's team, he had the opportunity to work with veteran NASCAR crew chief Ray Evernham. Gordon immediately felt comfortable with Evernham, who reminded him of his stepfather. Evernham, on the other hand, had serious doubts about the young driver. "The very first time I saw Jeff, he looked about 14 or 15 years old," Evernham recalls. "His mother was with him, and he had a briefcase in one hand. He called me Mr. Evernham. He was trying to grow a mustache, not very successfully, and when he opened his briefcase, he had a video game, a cell phone, and a racing magazine in it. I asked myself, 'What am I getting myself into?'"[13] Despite Evernham's reservations about the young driver, the two men worked well together during Gordon's brief stint with Connerty's race team.

When Connerty failed to line up a sponsor for his car for the 1991 Busch season, Gordon worried that he might not find another ride. Luckily for him, team owner Bill Davis ended up needing a driver after veteran Mark Martin left to form his own Busch team. Gordon drove Davis's Ford in thirty Busch races during the 1991 season. Although he struggled over the first half-dozen races, finishing no higher than 13th, he broke through in April to claim second place at the Nestle 200 at Lanier National Speedway in Georgia. Gordon showed consistent improvement from that point forward, and he ended the season with ten finishes in the Top 10. His performance was strong enough to earn Busch Series Rookie of the Year honors.

As the beginning of the 1992 season approached, Gordon convinced Davis to hire Evernham as his crew chief. The young driver knew that he would benefit from Evernham's organizational skills, experience, and guidance. Gordon appreciated his new crew chief's honest assessment of his driving performance, as well as his unparalleled ability to make technical adjustments to improve the car's performance. Thanks in part to Evernham's contributions, Gordon won three Busch races that year, notched fifteen finishes in the Top 10, and set a new NASCAR record by qualifying on the pole (in the first position, on the inside of the front row) eleven times. His results were good enough to rank fourth in the season point standings.

Gordon suited up as a driver in the Busch series in the early years of his NASCAR career, earning three wins in 1992.

Signs with Hendrick Motorsports

Gordon's strong performance during the 1992 Busch season caught the attention of many NASCAR insiders, including Winston Cup team owner Rick Hendrick. Hendrick watched Gordon compete in a Busch race at Atlanta Motor Speedway in Georgia and hold his own against a number of veteran Winston Cup drivers. He marveled at the young driver's ability to push his race car to the edge and yet still maintain control. "This white No. 1 car kept barreling through Turn 4 sideways," Hendrick remembers. "There was smoke coming off the tires, and I thought he'd get out of the throttle, but he just stood on the gas. I said, 'I'm going to stand here and watch this guy because he is going to bust his butt [crash].' But he did the same thing lap after lap and won the race. I just had to get that kid signed up."[14]

Upon meeting Gordon, Hendrick was equally impressed by his maturity. "I knew he had what it took," Hendrick says. "I figured I could get this incredible talent at a young age and mold him into a winning system."[15] Determined to add Gordon to his Hendrick Motorsports race team, Hendrick offered the young driver a contract before he had even lined up a car or a sponsor for him. Although Gordon was flattered, he initially resisted the idea of joining Hendrick Motorsports because he felt a sense of loyalty to Davis. A few months later, however, it became clear that Davis did not have the resources to move up to Winston Cup the following year. After ensuring that Evernham could come with him as his crew chief, Gordon signed a deal to race a Chevrolet for Hendrick Motorsports during the 1993 Winston Cup season.

When Gordon announced his decision to join Hendrick, many hard-core NASCAR fans were critical. Some people were upset that he had abandoned Davis, who had taken the risk of offering the rookie driver his first full-time ride. A number of other fans were outraged because Gordon's move meant that he switched car manufacturers, from Ford to Chevrolet. Many NASCAR fans feel intense loyalty to one automaker, and they view any driver who changes automakers to be a traitor. Finally, some people questioned the wisdom of Gordon's choice to join a team that was already running two other Winston Cup cars, driven by veterans

NASCAR Race Teams

NASCAR racing is a team sport. Race teams consist of dozens of people who make important contributions to the car's performance on the track. The team owner is the boss of the entire racing enterprise. The owner hires the driver and crew chief, and oversees the business operations of the race shop. An important part of the team

Rick Hendrick of Hendrick Motorsports is one of several prominent owners in the sport.

owner's job is to find corporate sponsors to help pay the high costs of maintaining a top-notch race team.

The main administrator under the owner is the team manager, who oversees the daily operations of the race shop. Among the team manager's responsibilities are ordering parts and equipment, hiring engineers and mechanics, and organizing test sessions. The crew chief is responsible for figuring out the best technical specifications for each track and ensuring that the race car is prepared in a way that will make it competitive. The crew chief decides everything from what adjustments to make to the suspension and bodywork, to how much air pressure to put in the tires, to how frequently to make pit stops. The driver must communicate well with the crew chief to provide information that helps improve the performance of the car.

A variety of other team members contribute to building and preparing specific parts of the car. These members include fabricators, engineers, mechanics, engine specialists, tire specialists, and parts specialists. The car chief oversees the work of these team members and ensures that they follow the crew chief's instructions. Finally, every race team includes a pit crew that travels to events, sets up and repairs the car as needed at the track, and refuels and changes tires on the car when it makes a pit stop during a race.

Ricky Rudd and Ken Schrader. At that time, most NASCAR teams consisted of a single car and driver. Campaigning multiple cars out of one race shop was a relatively new idea, and no team owner with more than one car had ever won a championship. Gordon ignored all the questions and criticism. He found the Hendrick Motorsports operation to be professionally run, with cutting-edge technology and outstanding resources, and felt that his new team gave him a great opportunity to succeed.

Moves Up to the Winston Cup Series

After Gordon finished out the Busch season for Davis, Hendrick arranged for him to make his Winston Cup debut in the final race of the 1992 season, the Hooters 500 at Atlanta Motor Speedway. It also happened to be the last race in the legendary career of seven-time NASCAR Winston Cup champion Richard Petty—known simply as "The King"—who had announced his plans to retire as a driver. Gordon was excited to be part of the new generation of drivers to build upon Petty's legacy as an ambassador for the sport of stock-car racing. "Richard set a bar for our sport that will never be matched," Gordon stated. "To have made my Winston Cup debut at his final race was a thrill."[16] Unfortunately for Gordon, taking to the track with Petty was his only thrill of the day. After qualifying 21st, he crashed early in the race and finished 31st.

Despite his less-than-stellar debut, Gordon felt optimistic as his first full Winston Cup season got underway in February 1993. The first race of every NASCAR season is also the biggest and most prestigious event in stock-car racing: the Daytona 500. Known as the "Great American Race," the Daytona 500 is preceded by several hotly contested qualifying races that do not count toward the season standings. Driving a rainbow-colored No. 24 Chevrolet Monte Carlo sponsored by DuPont, Gordon shocked everyone by winning the first 125-mile (201km) qualifying race, beating many top Winston Cup drivers in the process. After taking his victory lap, though, he appeared uncertain about what to do. He later admitted that he did not know the location of

Victory Lane, where winning drivers go to receive their trophies and give postrace interviews. Gordon proved that his victory was no fluke a few days later, when he finished an impressive fifth in his first career Daytona 500.

Gordon posted several more strong finishes during his rookie season, including second place in both the Coca-Cola 600 at Charlotte Motor Speedway in North Carolina and the Miller 400 at Richmond International Speedway in Virginia. He finished the season with eleven finishes in the Top 10, which placed him thir-

Gordon races his No. 24 Chevrolet Monte Carlo in the Daytona 500 in February 1993, impressing many with his fifth-place finish.

teenth in the season point standings and allowed him to claim Winston Cup Rookie of the Year honors. Along with the solid performances, however, Gordon also showed some inconsistency during his rookie season. Mechanical problems and accidents forced him out of a number of races, resulting in finishes of 30th place or lower in eight races. He also struggled at times to adjust to the higher level of competition on the Winston Cup circuit, where there was very little difference between the cars, drivers, and crews of the top teams and the bottom teams.

Marries Miss Winston

As the 1994 Winston Cup season approached, Gordon was determined to improve upon his rookie performance. He was particularly eager to prove that he belonged in the big leagues by earning a race victory. "I knew we were right on the cusp of doing something special, but we hadn't gotten there yet," he says of his No. 24 crew. "Until we did, we were just a young team with a lot of promise."[17] Gordon achieved his goal in May by winning the Coca-Cola 600 at Charlotte Motor Speedway. His crew chief provided the key to the victory. Gordon sat in third place with laps remaining in the grueling, 400-lap event. Low on fuel, he and the other leaders needed to make one final pit stop in order to finish the race. The other teams changed all four tires on their cars, but Evernham decided to change only Gordon's two right-side tires, which tend to wear out more quickly because they are on the outside of the corners. Thanks to the shortened pit stop, Gordon returned to the track with an eight-second lead and held on for the win.

Gordon chalked up a second victory that summer at the inaugural Brickyard 400 at Indianapolis Motor Speedway in Indiana. The 1994 event marked the first time that stock cars were allowed to race on the storied track that had long hosted the Indianapolis 500, and its $3.2 million purse was the largest in NASCAR history. The final 30 laps of the race featured an intense duel between Gordon and Winston Cup Series points leader Ernie Irvan. When Irvan cut a tire with a few laps remaining, Gordon was assured of the win. The second-year driver ended up a respectable eighth in

Gordon kisses fiancée Brooke Sealey, a former Miss Winston, after his Brickyard 400 victory at Indianapolis Motor Speedway in August 1994. The couple married the following November.

the season standings, with fourteen finishes in the Top 10, and half of those in the Top 5. He continued to show a bit of inconsistency, however, failing to complete ten races due to crashes and mechanical problems.

At the conclusion of the 1994 Winston Cup season, Gordon made headlines with personal news. He announced his engagement to Brooke Sealey, a psychology major at the University of North Carolina who also worked as a model. In 1993 Sealey was Miss Winston, which involved serving as a public relations spokesperson for Winston Cup sponsors at NASCAR races and other events. Her duties included greeting drivers at postrace Victory Lane ceremonies. Gordon first met Sealey during his rookie season, when she presented him with the trophy for winning the 125-mile Daytona qualifying race. Since NASCAR drivers are not allowed to socialize with Miss Winston away from the racetrack, the couple dated secretly for nearly two years. Whenever they both appeared at NASCAR awards banquets or promotional events, they went out of their way to avoid each other. They finally went public with their relationship after Sealey's term as Miss Winston ended. Gordon and Sealey married on November 26, 1994, and bought a home near Charlotte, North Carolina. From that time on, Brooke Gordon became an active and visible member of her husband's race team.

Chapter 3

Becoming a Champion

As Gordon prepared for his third Winston Cup season in 1995, he had high hopes of making a serious run at the championship. With two victories the previous year, he had already demonstrated that he had the ability to win races. Due to a combination of mechanical breakdowns and accidents, however, he had also failed to finish twenty-one races over the course of his first two Winston Cup seasons. His main priority for 1995 was to improve his consistency, since the NASCAR point system rewards drivers for finishing well week after week.

Gordon had a poor start, posting a disappointing 22nd-place finish in the season-opening Daytona 500. But he came back strong to win a remarkable three out of the next five races. He also showed admirable consistency by finishing among the Top 3 in five consecutive events. "This was one of those rolls, the kind of unexplainable streak where everybody on the team does everything right, and all the breaks seem to go our way,"[18] he said. Gordon experienced a bit of a lull in late May and early June. He returned to form later in the summer, however, when he won four more races and placed among the Top 8 finishers in fourteen consecutive events. In the meantime, he posted "did not finish" (DNF) results in only three races all year.

Establishes a Rivalry with Earnhardt

As the season wound down, Gordon appeared almost certain to claim his first Winston Cup title. His main rival for the crown was veteran driver Dale Earnhardt, a seven-time champion and a huge fan favorite. Driving the black No. 3 Chevrolet, Earnhardt had gained a reputation as a tough competitor and a master of the old-school, fender-rubbing style of stock-car racing. His aggressive style on the track had earned him such nicknames as "The Intimidator" and "The Man in Black." Many NASCAR fans were upset at the prospect of a young newcomer upstaging their hero and preventing Earnhardt from becoming the only driver in history to win eight Winston Cup titles. "I guess a lot of fans took exception to a 23-year-old nudging The Intimidator out of first place,"[19] Gordon acknowledged.

Gordon led Earnhardt by 302 points with four races remaining. By the time the two drivers arrived in Hampton, Georgia, for the

Legendary driver Dale Earnhardt, driving his No. 3 car in front of Gordon at a race at Talladega Speedway in April 1995, became Gordon's main rival for the Winston Cup title that season.

Confronting Anti-Gordon Sentiments

Although Jeff Gordon attracted millions of new fans to NASCAR, some old-time, stock-car racing fans did not like him. Traditionally, NASCAR drivers came from the American South, grew up racing stock cars, and had a tough-guy image. Gordon has California roots, a background in open-wheel racing, and a clean-cut image and that made him unacceptable to some fans. In fact, the more successful Gordon became on the track, the less popular he became among a certain segment of NASCAR fans.

Gordon tried not to let the negative attention bother him. On a few occasions, he even turned it into an excuse to be silly and have fun. One time, Gordon joined fellow drivers Elliott Sadler and Jimmie Johnson for a joyride in a golf cart around the Watkins Glen road course in upstate New York. As they drove through the spectator paddock, they noticed a converted school bus that was covered with anti-Gordon slogans and photos. The owner of the vehicle stood outside expressing anti-Gordon sentiments through a bullhorn.

The NASCAR drivers were suddenly inspired to stop for a visit. As the owner of the bus looked on in amazement, Gordon posed for pictures in front of it and autographed some anti-Gordon posters. Then he and his friends drove away laughing.

final race of the season, Earnhardt had cut the margin to 147 points. But Gordon still controlled his own destiny. He only needed to finish better than 41st or to lead a lap in order to claim the title. While Gordon struggled with a poorly handling car, Earnhardt led 268 laps and won the race. Gordon, however, still managed to lead a lap by remaining on the track while most of his competitors made pit stops. He thus won the Winston Cup championship by 34 points in just his third year competing on the circuit.

At twenty-four years old, Gordon became the youngest champion in modern NASCAR history. Earnhardt, who was twenty years his senior, joked afterward that the young driver would probably have to celebrate his title with a glass of milk instead of with the traditional champagne. Gordon played along with the joke at the annual NASCAR awards banquet, when he reached into an ice bucket and pulled out a bottle of milk to drink a toast to his rival.

Challenges NASCAR's Point System

Winning the 1995 Winston Cup championship lifted Gordon to a whole new level of fame, media attention, and public scrutiny. He was interviewed for countless magazine and newspaper articles, appeared as a guest on such television programs as *The Late Show with David Letterman* and *Good Morning America*, and signed several lucrative new endorsement deals. All the attention he received gave Gordon a much higher profile at the beginning of the 1996 Winston Cup season. Rather than being viewed as a talented but unproven young driver, he was now the defending champion and the man to beat.

Gordon continued to outclass most of his rivals in 1996. He won an amazing ten races, including three in a row in September. Unfortunately, he also posted six finishes of 30th place or lower over the course of the season, and his inconsistency ended up hurting his chances to repeat as Winston Cup champion. Fellow Hendrick Motorsports driver Terry Labonte only won two races that year, but he also notched twenty-two Top 5 finishes and placed lower than 30th in only one race. Gordon trailed Labonte by 47 points going into the final race of the season, the NAPA 500 at Atlanta Motor Speedway in Georgia. Gordon made a valiant bid to defend his crown by finishing third in the event. But Labonte finished fifth, which allowed him to clinch the Winston Cup title by a razor-thin margin of 37 points.

Although Gordon was disappointed not to win the championship himself, he was pleased that the Hendrick Motorsports team had achieved two in a row. He felt that Labonte's victory had proven the value of Hendrick's innovative approach to racing, in which multiple race teams operated out of one facility. Not everyone was satisfied with the season's outcome, however.

Gordon celebrates his first Winston Cup title in 1995. Although he won ten races the following year, he finished second in points and lost the title to Terry Labonte.

Many fans felt that Gordon's ten victories proved that he was the dominant driver in 1996 and deserved to win the championship. The fact that Labonte had claimed the title despite winning only two races led to criticism of NASCAR's point system.

Wins Back-to-Back Championships

As the start of the 1997 NASCAR season approached, Gordon learned that team owner Rick Hendrick was battling leukemia, a form of cancer that affects the blood cells. While Hendrick was undergoing treatment, he was too weak to work at the race shop or travel to racetracks. The Hendrick Motorsports team made a special effort to have a successful season in order to raise the spirits of their leader. Gordon promised Hendrick a victory in the season-opening Daytona 500, and he delivered. To make the day complete, his Hendrick Motorsports teammates Terry Labonte and Ricky Craven finished second and third, respectively.

NASCAR Tracks

NASCAR races take place on four different types of tracks: short ovals that are less than 1 mile (1.6km) in length; intermediate ovals that are between 1 and 2 miles (1.6km and 3.2km) in length; superspeedways that are longer than 2 miles (3.2km) in length; and road courses that are anywhere between 2 and 4 miles (3.2 and 6.4km).

The Homestead-Miami Speedway is one of the intermediate-oval tracks on the NASCAR circuit.

Road courses require drivers to make both left- and right-hand turns, whereas ovals are driven counterclockwise and consist of only left-hand turns. Most NASCAR race teams have different cars that are specifically set up to run on each type of track.

The two fastest superspeedways, Daytona International Speedway in Florida, and Talladega Superspeedway in Alabama, are known as restrictor-plate tracks. NASCAR rules require the cars that race there to be equipped with restrictor plates—special devices that reduce air flow to the engine and limit the top speed of the car—with the goal of increasing driver safety. Some NASCAR drivers complain, however, that restrictor plates actually make the races more dangerous by forcing cars to run in large groups and thus increasing the risk of multivehicle accidents.

Gordon sprays champagne to celebrate his third Winston Cup victory after winning the NAPA 500 race at Atlanta Motor Speedway in November 1998.

Gordon went on to win nine more races in 1997 and post a total of twenty-three finishes in the Top 5. The competition for the Winston Cup championship remained close, however, because Gordon also finished lower than 20th place in seven events. In fact, Gordon was one of three drivers—along with Mark Martin and Dale Jarrett—who had a chance to clinch the title at the final race of the season in Atlanta, Georgia. A nervous Gordon nearly took himself out of the running by crashing in the pit lane during a prerace practice. Although he only managed to finish 17th in his backup car, he squeaked through to claim his second career Winston Cup championship by 14 points.

In contrast, the outcome of the 1998 season was never in doubt. As the campaign unfolded, Gordon turned in one of the most dominant performances in NASCAR history. He posted an incredible thirteen victories to tie the record set by Richard Petty in 1975. He looked completely unstoppable during the summer months, when he won six out of seven races, including a streak of four in a row. Gordon ended the season with an unprecedented twenty-six finishes in the Top 5 out of thirty-three events. He compiled the highest point total in NASCAR history, with 5,328, to claim his third career Winston Cup championship by 364 points over Mark Martin. Gordon topped off his record-setting year by becoming the first NASCAR driver ever to earn more than $9 million in prize money during a single season.

Increases the Popularity of NASCAR

From his first Winston Cup championship season in 1995 to his third in 1998, Gordon won an amazing forty races and claimed a spot among the best drivers in the history of stock-car racing. Whenever he was asked about the secret of his success, though, he gave most of the credit to crew chief Ray Evernham, team owner

Fans gather around Gordon in hopes of an autograph at the Daytona USA attraction in 1999. Gordon is credited in part with bringing the sport into the mainstream and boosting its popularity in the 1990s.

Rick Hendrick, and the entire Hendrick Motorsports operation. "It was the team that made us what we were,"[20] he explains.

As the most visible member of that team, though, Gordon received most of the attention from NASCAR fans and the media. His emergence as the dominant force in stock-car racing, as well as his popularity and personal appeal, were widely credited with updating the image of NASCAR and expanding its fan base nationwide. "With his movie-star looks, beauty-queen wife and an all-American image, Gordon is on track to become auto racing's reigning superstar in the next millennium,"[21] declares writer Roland Lazenby in an article in *Sport* magazine.

Gordon's California roots, open-wheel racing background, and clean-cut image represented a major change from old-style NASCAR drivers. Most previous Winston Cup champions had hailed from the South, grown up racing stock cars, and cultivated a tough-guy image that embraced the sport's outlaw past. Partly because he was so different from the traditional NASCAR drivers, Gordon helped attract a legion of new fans to NASCAR racing. "Jeff has been one of those people who changed what a race car driver is," fellow driver Jeff Burton explained to ESPN. "Look at Richard Petty. Look at Dale Earnhardt. Look at Cale Yarborough. Then look at Jeff Gordon. That's not the same picture. Jeff helped bring mainstream young America into our sport."[22]

Thanks in part to Gordon's influence, NASCAR grew tremendously during the 1990s. It signed up big-name sponsors, added more races and new tracks, expanded television coverage, and increased revenues. "For NASCAR," writer Jerry Adler explains in *Newsweek*, "Gordon represents a breakthrough, a vindication of its long effort to transcend its barefoot origins as a contest between Southern sheriffs and moonshiners."[23]

Experiences a Backlash

Of course, not everyone appreciated the changes that Gordon brought to NASCAR. As the sport grew in popularity during the 1990s, some longtime fans felt that it lost touch with its roots and became too bland and commercial. Since NASCAR

The checkered flag waves as Gordon crosses the finish line under a caution at the debris-covered track at Talladega Speedway in 2004. Anti-Gordon spectators threw bottles and other litter to protest a controversial call that put Gordon in the lead.

promoted Gordon heavily as a three-time champion, many old-school NASCAR fans blamed him for "ruining" the sport. Critics complained that he did not fit with the grassroots racing tradition and rural Southern "good old boy" image that had long served as the basis for NASCAR's appeal. They viewed him as a privileged California pretty boy who did not have to work for his success. "I didn't smoke, didn't chew tobacco, didn't go deer hunting, and would rather dive with a school of fish than sit in a boat and catch them," Gordon explains. "The more I won, the more fans I attracted, and the more people pulled against me."[24]

A few people, tired of watching Gordon dominate the competition week after week, began booing him enthusiastically and wearing T-shirts that read "Anyone But Gordon." In fact, Gordon became a polarizing force within NASCAR nation, attracting some of the most devoted supporters as well as some of the most vocal detractors. Gordon tried to ignore the negative crowd reactions and focus on going fast and winning races. Some of his opponents praised the way he handled himself in the face of anti-Gordon sentiment. "I am, in a lot of ways, a Jeff Gordon fan," fellow driver Mark Martin told *Sports Illustrated* magazine in 1998. "I approve of him, the way he lives his life, the way he conducts himself, and everything else. If the fans who don't like Jeff Gordon—if they think they don't like him, well, they should just imagine how a different personality could be in his situation. It hurts me to hear him booed because he's good."[25]

Chapter 4

Winning with a New Team

Jeff Gordon delighted his fans—and disappointed his detractors—by starting off the 1999 season with an exciting, come-from-behind victory in the prestigious Daytona 500. Although Gordon qualified on the pole, he received a fifteen-second penalty for having too many crew members over the wall at one time during a pit stop. The penalty dropped him to last place among the pack of cars on the lead lap. Gordon gradually worked his way through the field to reach third place with eleven laps remaining. He then caught a draft behind Dale Earnhardt that enabled him to move up to second place. The two drivers engaged in a classic duel for several laps until Gordon managed to cross the finish line first and take the checkered flag (the flag that is waved as the winner crosses the finish line). Gordon went on to win six more races that season and post a total of eighteen finishes in the Top 5. But he also struggled with inconsistency, finishing 30th or lower in eight events, which relegated him to a disappointing sixth place in the season point standings.

Loses Crew Chief

Many NASCAR insiders attributed Gordon's problems to the upheaval that was occurring behind the scenes at Hendrick Motorsports during the 1999 season. From the time that Gordon claimed his third Winston Cup title in 1998, his longtime crew chief, Ray Evernham, had indicated a desire to move on and seek

The Life of a NASCAR Driver

Jeff Gordon and other NASCAR drivers spend a great deal of time away from home. In addition to testing cars and making promotional appearances for sponsors, they travel to races thirty-six weekends per year. On a typical race weekend, Gordon flies to the track on Thursday for practice and qualifying sessions. His race car and other equipment travels separately in a specially equipped semitrailer. At the track, Gordon stays in a 45-foot (14m) motor coach with a bedroom, kitchen, shower, and television.

On the day of the race, Gordon attends a morning drivers' meeting to go over the rules and special instructions for that event and track. He also attends religious services at the track chapel. Next, Gordon usually spends some time visiting the hospitality tents set up by DuPont and other major sponsors. After signing autographs for some of the hundreds of fans who line the garage and pit areas, he makes his way to the Hendrick Motorsports trailer to get ready for the race.

Gordon's prerace ritual includes changing into his driver's suit, eating a light lunch, doing some stretching, and visualizing his race strategy. He also holds a brief prerace meeting with his pit crew. Finally, Gordon makes his way to pit row, listens to the national anthem, and climbs into his car through the window (There are no functioning doors on a race car. They are considered a safety hazard so drivers climb in through a window). After attaching his steering wheel, buckling his safety harness, and putting on his helmet, he checks all of his instruments and switches and waits to hear the command, "Drivers, start your engines!"

new challenges as a team owner. As Evernham explored various opportunities, his future—and Gordon's—became the subject of intense media speculation. The questions and uncertainty created an unwanted distraction for the No. 24 team throughout the 1999 campaign.

Ray Evernham, right, Gordon's longtime crew chief, parted ways with Hendrick Motorsports in 1999 to pursue ownership of a Busch series team. Some blamed Gordon's inconsistent performance that year on the distraction of Evernham's departure.

Gordon freely acknowledges the important role Evernham played in his phenomenal success. "Ideally our roles should be 50-50," Gordon says of the relationship between driver and crew chief.

> From one standpoint, the danger I put myself in as a driver might make my part more than that. But when it comes down to pure competition, to how well I'm going to do in a race, I don't know if I'm even 50 percent of the combination. That car comes off the truck so well prepared that I can get in, go out for the first two or three laps of practice and say, "Yeaaahhh!"[26]

Midway through the 1999 season, Evernham officially announced that he would leave Hendrick Motorsports to form his own Busch team for the 2000 season. He made an arrangement with the automobile manufacturer DaimlerChrysler to oversee the return of the Dodge brand to NASCAR after a twenty-year absence. Evernham invited Gordon to join his new race team, but the driver opted to remain with Hendrick Motorsports. Gordon had signed a lifetime contract with Hendrick that gave him part ownership of the team. "Ray and I had been friends, partners, team members, and champions. We had been to the top of the mountain together," Gordon explained. "Now it was time to go our separate ways."[27]

Enters a Rebuilding Phase

As the start of the 2000 Winston Cup season approached, many NASCAR insiders expressed doubts about Gordon's chances to win another championship. Critics pointed out that Evernham had set up the 24 car and made all the important decisions for the team, and they claimed that Gordon had been happy to defer to his crew chief's judgment. "Evernham hired the crew, crafted the race strategy and was always the loudest voice in team meetings," sportswriter Lars Anderson wrote in *Sports Illustrated*. "So when Evernham suddenly left Hendrick Motorsports ... it was as if the 24 team had been lobotomized [a surgical procedure that removes part of the brain]."[28] Some people predicted that Gordon would have trouble winning without Evernham. "I give most of the credit for Jeff's success to Ray Evernham," said rival team owner Junior Johnson in 1998. "I think if you put Jeff in some other car and put somebody else in Evernham's car, you'd see."[29]

To make matters worse for Gordon, many members of his race team left with Evernham. He started the 2000 season with a new crew chief, Robbie Loomis—who came to Hendrick from Petty Enterprises with a personal recommendation from NASCAR legend Richard Petty—as well as an entirely new pit crew. Naturally, it took some time for the new 24 team to learn to work together effectively. "People who expected us to come out and win a lot of races right off the bat either didn't know our sport or they were fooling themselves,"[30] Gordon explains.

The fact that Gordon's team had entered a rebuilding phase became clear at the Daytona 500, when his engine failed and

Gordon and his team members pose in Victory Lane with the trophy for winning the DieHard 500 at Talladega Superspeedway in April 2000. This was the 50th victory of his career.

he finished 34th. Gordon still managed to win three races in 2000, including the Diehard 500 at Talladega Superspeedway in Alabama, which marked the 50th victory of his career. But he performed inconsistently for much of the season and ended up finishing ninth in the point standings—the worst result since his rookie year.

Still, there were some signs that things were looking up for Gordon and the 24 team. They learned from their mistakes and showed gradual improvement, finishing in the Top 10 in ten out of the last eleven races of the season. Over the course of the difficult 2000 campaign, Gordon steadily increased his involvement and took charge of the race team. Even his former crew chief noticed the difference. "Jeff has been ready to be a leader for some time," Evernham told *Sports Illustrated*. "Jeff and I first got together when he was 18. My role was to be the mentor, and he was the student. But he doesn't need a mentor anymore. He always was the key to his team's success and now, finally, I think he realizes that."[31] As the 24 team prepared for the 2001 season, though, it remained to be seen whether it could return to the top under Gordon's leadership.

Bids Farewell to His Rival

The 2001 Winston Cup season started off on a tragic note. On the last lap of the Daytona 500, NASCAR legend Dale Earnhardt crashed into the wall in Turn 4. He died instantly from severe head and neck injuries. Earnhardt's death sent shock waves through NASCAR nation. For Gordon, who was knocked out of the race with twenty-two laps remaining and finished 30th, the incident offered a valuable reminder about the important things in life. "It's things like losing Dale that make you think about how precious life is," he explained. "You need to live every minute as if it could be your last."[32]

From the beginning of Gordon's career, the media had always presented him and Earnhardt as bitter rivals. The two drivers did provide an intriguing study in contrasts: Earnhardt as the gritty veteran and Gordon as the young hotshot. Earnhardt often seemed to enjoy fanning the flames of the rivalry by teasing

Gordon, left, and Dale Earnhardt chat during a break from practice at Talladega Superspeedway in 1997. Although the media made them out to be bitter rivals, in reality they were good friends.

Gordon and calling him "Wonder Boy." In reality, though, the two drivers respected each other and got along fine. "Dale and I were friends and business partners," Gordon said. "We didn't hunt and fish together, but we ... were close."[33]

As the world of NASCAR struggled to recover from the loss of a legend, a national tragedy further disrupted the 2001 season. On September 11, terrorists hijacked four airliners and crashed them into the World Trade Center in New York,

NASCAR Safety

Although accidents occur fairly often during NASCAR races, serious injuries are rare thanks to the safety equipment required for cars and drivers. For example, stock cars feature a roll cage made of strong metal tubing that surrounds the cockpit and protects the driver. In addition, the driver

Dale Earnhardt Jr. puts on his racing helmet equipped with a head and neck support (HANS) device.

sits in a specially molded seat that holds the body securely and wears a five-point restraint system made of sturdy nylon straps. NASCAR drivers also wear special racing suits made of fire-retardant materials and padded helmets with hard shells to protect their heads. Finally, NASCAR requires drivers to use a head and neck support (HANS) device to prevent whiplash injuries.

These precautions are necessary because anyone who drives a race car at speeds of over 180 miles per hour (290 kmh) will eventually be involved in a crash. Jeff Gordon explains how it feels when he loses control of his car:

> That's the only time fear really comes into play as a driver. You don't know what the outcome will be, how much it is going to hurt or whether you are going to survive. You see the wall coming, but you have no time to react. Your heart rate goes from nothing to through the roof in a split second. When it's over you are checking your limbs and looking around, like, wow!

Quoted in Elizabeth Newman, "Jeff Gordon." *Sports Illustrated*, July 31, 2006. p. 28.

the Pentagon in Virginia, and a field in Pennsylvania. Nearly three thousand people died. Out of respect for the victims of the attacks and their families, NASCAR canceled the race that had been scheduled for the following weekend. When Gordon and the other Winston Cup drivers returned to action on September 23, they paid their respects by holding a moment of silence before the race and displaying the American flag on all of their cars.

Wins Fourth Winston Cup Title

Despite all the adversity, Gordon managed to have a strong season in 2001. He qualified on the pole in seven events, posted six victories, and finished in the Top 10 in twenty-four out of thirty-six races. His results were good enough to return him to the top of the Winston Cup point standings at the end of the season. Gordon thus earned the fourth championship of his career in only his ninth full year competing on the circuit. He became the third driver in NASCAR history to win four career championships, and the only one to accomplish this feat by the age of thirty. The only men with more Winston Cup trophies were Richard Petty and Dale Earnhardt, who each claimed seven titles in their long careers.

In many ways, Gordon found his fourth championship to be the most satisfying of all. He had not only proven that he could win without Evernham, but he had also contributed to the team's success in more ways than before. As a part owner of the 24 team, Gordon had made more of the decisions relating to the technical preparation of the car. He had also played a larger role in selecting, leading, and motivating his crew members. His increased participation gave him a new appreciation for what it took to win. "I've had more input in assembling this team than I've had since the days when my stepfather and I traveled the country towing a sprint car,"[34] Gordon acknowledges.

At the annual NASCAR awards banquet, Gordon was also gratified to receive the 2001 True Value Man of the Year Award for his charitable activities. Through the Jeff Gordon Children's

Gordon hugs team owner Rick Hendrick, left, to celebrate winning his fourth Winston Cup in 2001.

Foundation, which he established in 1999, Gordon raised more than $7 million to help children battling cancer. The foundation funds medical research toward discovering a cure, treatment programs to increase survival rates, and programs to improve patients' quality of life. It also provides support to the Jeff Gordon Children's Hospital, a state-of-the-art pediatric cancer treatment facility in Concord, North Carolina. Gordon looked back on his accomplishments in NASCAR—which now included four

Winston Cup championships, fifty-eight career wins, and a total of $45 million in prize money—with great satisfaction. "It's been such a flash," he said at the time. "I have done some things that have been incredible. I never dreamed I'd be in this position. If the next 10 years are as good as these past 10, I'm not going to know what to do."[35]

Chapter 5

Maturing as a Driver and Team Owner

Following Jeff Gordon's fourth Winston Cup championship, Hendrick Motorsports decided to launch a fourth cup team for the 2002 season. The new No. 48 Lowe's Chevrolet joined the No. 24 DuPont car driven by Gordon, the No. 5 Kellogg's Frosted Flakes car driven by Terry Labonte, and the No. 25 United Auto Workers/Delphi Auto Parts car driven by Jerry Nadeau. All four cars were built, prepared, and maintained by the five hundred employees of Hendrick Motorsports's state-of-the-art race shop in Charlotte, North Carolina. Although each car had its own dedicated crew, the teams shared technical information, research findings, and race strategies. Gordon made an agreement to co-own the new car with team owner Rick Hendrick. Gordon's first responsibility as an owner of the 48 team was to find a driver.

Hires Jimmie Johnson

As it turned out, the driver found him. Gordon was sitting in the Hendrick Motorsports race trailer at Michigan International Speedway when a young Busch Series driver knocked on the door. Jimmie Johnson introduced himself, explained that he had just lost his sponsor, and asked Gordon to help him figure

Jimmie Johnson, left, celebrates with teammate Gordon after winning the pole position for the Daytona 500 in 2002. This was the first of several accomplishments for Johnson in his outstanding rookie season.

out his next career move. "I went to Jeff and said, 'Hey, do you have any advice? What should I be looking out for myself?'" Johnson recalled. "He said, 'You're not gonna believe this, but we're interested in starting a fourth Winston Cup team in 2002, and we want you to possibly drive that car.' I was like, 'What did you say?' It was so amazing to go in looking for some advice and walk out of the back of that truck thinking I might have a shot at a Winston Cup ride."[36]

After discussing the choice with Rick Hendrick, Gordon made Johnson an offer to drive the 48 car for the 2002 season. The decision shocked many NASCAR analysts and race fans. Since Gordon and Hendrick could have had their pick of the best racers available, they wondered why the partners chose a young, unproven driver like Johnson, who had only won one race in two full seasons in the Busch Series. Gordon believed that Johnson had more talent than his results indicated. "I don't want to knock his Busch car, but I knew he'd be better when he got stuff he could drive straight," Gordon said. "Plus I raced him [in a 2000 Busch race] in Michigan, and he beat me."[37] Gordon also felt comfortable with Johnson from the time they first met. "He impressed me. He was the guy I wanted," he explained. "We hit it off from the beginning. I knew that's why he'd fit so well. I knew it was going to be a team that was under the same roof as the 24 and that those people had to work really well together and the drivers had to work really close together."[38]

Johnson soon proved that Gordon's confidence in him was well-founded. The rookie burst onto the Winston Cup scene in 2002 by qualifying on the pole at the season-opening Daytona 500. After posting Top 10 finishes in six of the first twelve races of the season, Johnson earned his first Winston Cup victory in just his thirteenth career start. Gordon, by contrast, had not managed to win a race until well into his second Winston Cup season. Johnson ended his spectacular rookie year with three victories and an impressive fifth-place finish in the point standings. His success pleased Gordon and everyone at Hendrick Motorsports.

Goes Through a Divorce

As Johnson established himself as one of the top competitors on the Winston Cup circuit, Gordon entered a rough patch in both his career and his personal life. Gordon's wife of eight years, Brooke, filed for divorce in February 2002, at the start of the NASCAR race season. As part of the settlement, she asked for their mansion in Florida and a large share of Gordon's $50 million in career earnings. The divorce turned bitter and dragged on for sixteen months. During that time, Gordon was frequently the subject of dramatic tell-all feature stories in tabloid magazines. Although he tried to keep his personal life separate from his racing career, the whole situation proved to be a terrible distraction for him. "In hindsight the divorce drained me," he admitted, "and it showed up in my 2002 performance."[39]

The defending champion got off to a slow start in 2002 and struggled with inconsistency all season. Including the last few

Gordon's oceanfront mansion in Florida and other aspects of his private life were discussed in the tabloids when he split from wife Brooke in 2002.

events of 2001, Gordon endured a thirty-one-race winless streak before breaking through for back-to-back victories at Bristol Motor Speedway in Tennessee and Darlington Raceway in North Carolina. He added a third win later in the season at Kansas Speedway in Kansas to give him twenty finishes in the Top 10 for the year. Since he also finished lower than fifteenth place in thirteen events, however, he ended up a disappointing fourth in the Winston Cup point standings—only one spot ahead of his rookie teammate.

Although Gordon's messy divorce had a negative impact on his performance as a driver, it seemed to have a more positive impact on his personal life. By many accounts, Gordon felt less pressure to maintain his squeaky-clean image and more freedom to loosen up and be himself in the wake of all the splashy tabloid coverage. "We're seeing a new Jeff," said David Poole, a motor-sports writer for the *Charlotte Observer* and a close friend of Gordon.

He's now less-guarded, more open with people. The single biggest change I see in Jeff is that—maybe for the first time in his life—he is doing things in a way he thinks is best for him. It used to be that he did everything to try please other people.... He's still a great guy, but when someone goes through major changes in his life the way he has in the past year or so, he can't help but be affected.[40]

Gordon demonstrated his new attitude when he hosted the classic late-night sketch-comedy television series *Saturday Night Live* before the start of the 2003 Winston Cup season. He was the first race-car driver ever invited to serve as the show's celebrity host. Gordon performed in a series of silly skits with the show's cast of comedians. In one humorous bit, he portrayed a NASCAR fan in a mullet wig and engaged in a mock fistfight with actor Gary Busey. "I think I'm just sort of maturing, coming out of my shell a little bit," Gordon explained. "I've learned from good decisions I've made and bad decisions I've made, and I'm trying to be more myself than I ever have before. I don't feel like I have really changed. Maybe I have let people see more of me than in the past."[41]

Faces Stiffer Competition

Gordon's stint on *Saturday Night Live* reflected the continued growth of NASCAR's popularity. Thanks in part to Gordon's appeal, stock-car racing expanded its reach nationwide to an estimated 75 million devoted fans. Attendance at races increased to an average of more than 130,000 spectators per event, and millions more people tuned in to race coverage on television, making NASCAR the second most-watched sport on American TV after professional football. NASCAR fans spent more than $1 billion each year to buy clothing and other merchandise bearing the name, car number, or image of their favorite drivers. High-profile corporate sponsors clamored to associate themselves with popular drivers and place their logos on cars and race suits.

The tremendous growth of NASCAR during the late 1990s and early 2000s also attracted a new crop of talented drivers to

NASCAR fans check out T-shirts and other merchandise featuring their favorite drivers and cars at a souvenir stand. Gordon's fan appeal is credited in part with raising the sport's profile nationwide.

stock-car racing. The arrival of Jimmie Johnson and other young hotshots made the Winston Cup circuit more challenging for Gordon and other veterans. NASCAR also introduced new rules to eliminate differences between the cars and increase the level of competition. As a result, it became harder for any one driver to dominate and achieve double-digit victories in a season the way Gordon once did. "His position in the sport has changed," Poole acknowledged. "Jeff no longer is the one driver out in front. A lot more hot young drivers have come into the sport—getting great opportunities thanks mostly to Gordon—and that has taken a lot of pressure off of him. All of sudden the media has other stories to chase and the fans have other young drivers to boo/cheer."[42]

With greater equality among the competitors, Gordon once again finished fourth in the Winston Cup point standings in 2003. His season followed a similar pattern to the one before. Gordon performed inconsistently through the first half of the season and endured a twenty-three-race winless streak before breaking through for a victory at Bristol Motor Speedway in late August. Although he rebounded in the fall, winning two of the last nine races and finishing in the Top 10 eight times, it was not enough to overcome his six finishes of thirtieth place or lower. Meanwhile, his teammate Johnson turned in a remarkable performance for a second-year driver and ended the season ranked second in the point standings.

Narrowly Misses Winning Fifth Title

Prior to the start of the 2004 season, NASCAR's premier race series got a new sponsor and its name changed from Winston Cup to Nextel Cup. NASCAR also changed the point system that determines which driver earns the coveted cup championship. Instead of simply adding up each driver's points at the end of the thirty-six-race season, the organization instituted a ten-race playoff called the Chase for the Cup. Only the top twelve drivers in the point standings at the end of twenty-six races qualified to compete in the playoff. At that point, the twelve qualifiers had their points reset to five thousand, and they also received ten additional points for each victory in the first twenty-six races. During the ten-race Chase for the Cup, points were awarded as usual. This system effectively wiped out any big point leads that drivers accumulated, making the end of the season more exciting for fans. (A new, simpler points system was announced in January 2011 and instituted for the 2011 season.)

The new point system probably cost Gordon his fifth title in 2004. He won five races that season and sat comfortably atop the point standings at the end of twenty-six races. But his lead virtually disappeared when all the drivers' point totals were reset at the beginning of the playoff. Fellow driver Kurt Busch was more consistent than Gordon over the last ten races of the season, so he ended up claiming the championship by eight points over second-place finisher Jimmie Johnson. Gordon finished third, sixteen points behind Busch. The gritty but unsuccessful title bids by Gordon and Johnson were a big disappointment to Hendrick Motorsports, which had desperately wanted to capture

The 2011 NASCAR Point System

In 2011 a new scoring system was put into effect for the three national series in NASCAR—the Sprint Cup, the Nationwide Series, and the Truck Series. NASCAR drivers receive 43 points for winning a race, 42 points for finishing second, 41 for finishing third, and so on down to forty-third (last) place. The last-place driver in each Sprint Cup and Nationwide Series race received 1 point, while last place in each Truck Series race receives 8 points. The winning driver receives 3 bonus points. Drivers can earn an additional 1 point for leading a lap during a race, plus 1 more point for leading the most laps during a race. The maximum number of points a driver can earn in a single race is 48, assuming that he or she finishes first and leads more laps than any other driver.

The All-American Series still uses the old points system. Drivers receive 185 points for winning a race, 170 points for finishing second, 165 for finishing third, and so on down to forty-third (last) place, which is worth 34 points. Drivers can earn an additional 5 points for leading a lap during a race, plus 5 more points for leading the most laps during a race. The maximum number of points a driver can earn in a single race is 195, assuming that he or she finishes first and leads more laps than any other driver.

the championship that year as a way of honoring ten Hendrick family members and employees who were killed in a plane crash in October 2004. Among those who lost their lives was team owner Rick Hendrick's twenty-four-year-old son, Ricky.

Gordon started off the 2005 season with a bang by winning the prestigious Daytona 500 for the third time in his career. He managed to avoid several late accidents that knocked out multiple competitors, then sealed the victory by making a daring pass of Dale Earnhardt Jr., the son of his former rival. "Those are the moments you live for," he said afterward. "Those are the moments we get paid the big bucks for. You live to be in that position—to have chaos happening all around you and to have your car lead the pack."[43]

Gordon crosses the finish line for the win at the 2005 Daytona 500. Despite success early in the season, he failed to qualify for the Chase for the Cup that year.

Steve Letarte

Born in Maine in 1979, Steve Letarte grew up watching his father, Don, drive race cars on tracks throughout New England. Their love of racing brought both father and son to North Carolina to work for Hendrick Motorsports. While Don built chassis, sixteen-year-old Steve swept floors in the race shop and followed various crew members around asking questions. "Steve asked, like, 900 questions a day," recalls Robbie Loomis, who spent five years as Jeff Gordon's crew chief. "He never, ever stopped with the questions."

Steve Letarte joined Hendrick Motorsports as a mechanic and tire specialist in 1996; nine years later, he became Gordon's crew chief.

In 1996 the inquisitive young man got a full-time job at Hendrick as a mechanic and tire specialist for the 24 team. He was promoted to car chief in 2002 and to crew chief in 2005, at the age of twenty-six. "As a young guy Steve could dissect what I was saying and get a mental picture of what was happening in the car," Gordon says.

After five years together, Gordon and Letarte parted ways at the end of the 2010 season. Hendrick Motorsports announced that Letarte would serve as crew chief for the 88 car driven by Dale Earnhardt Jr. beginning in 2011. Alan Gustafson, who had previously served as crew chief for the 5 car driven by Mark Martin, took over that role on Gordon's team.

Quoted in Lars Anderson, "Here Comes Mr. Gordon." *Sports Illustrated*, July 2, 2007. p. 64.

The exciting Daytona 500 victory was the beginning of a hot streak in which Gordon won three of the first nine races of the 2005 season. In the process he accomplished his seventieth career win, becoming the eighth driver in NASCAR history to reach that milestone. Just when it appeared that he may have regained his championship form, however, Gordon's luck took a sharp turn in the other direction. He finished in 30th place or lower in five of the next six races, and his season fell apart. To the shock of many NASCAR fans, he failed to qualify for the Chase for the Cup. "The bottom line is, we were way off, and we've got a lot of work to do,"[44] Gordon acknowledged at the time. The pressure became too much for his longtime crew chief, Robbie Loomis, who decided to move to a different position within the Hendrick Motorsports organization. Rick Hendrick chose twenty-six-year-old Steve Letarte to take over as Gordon's crew chief. NASCAR insiders eagerly awaited the 2006 season to see whether Letarte's fresh perspective could put Gordon back on top.

Chapter 6

Driving for a Fifth Championship

J eff Gordon immediately established a comfortable working relationship with his new crew chief, Steve Letarte. Letarte had worked in the Hendrick Motorsports race shop since the age of sixteen, and he had spent the previous few years serving as car chief (second in command under the crew chief) for Gordon's 24 team. "I won a lot of races with Ray Evernham, but I've never been around anyone who can get on the same page with me as fast as Steve,"[45] Gordon says. The personnel change did not pay off immediately, though, as Gordon continued to struggle with inconsistency during the 2006 Nextel Cup season. He chalked up two victories, but he only managed to place sixth in the point standings. Gordon experienced greater success as an owner, however, as Jimmie Johnson and the 48 team claimed their first Nextel Cup championship.

The real highlight of the year for Gordon was an event that took place away from the track. He married Belgian fashion model Ingrid Vandebosch on November 7, 2006. They first met in 2003, while Gordon was still recovering from his divorce, and became friends. When they finally began dating in 2005, Gordon's family was delighted. "Ingrid is the first person that Jeff has ever been around who actually understands him," says his stepfather, John Bickford. "He's not afraid to be himself anymore, imperfections and all. Ingrid is funny, well-educated, worldly, and she brought out this whole new side to Jeff."[46] A few months after the wedding, Gordon and Vandebosch announced

Gordon and Belgian fashion model Ingrid Vandebosch attend the NASCAR awards ceremony in December 2006 after getting married the month before.

that they were expecting their first child. Their daughter, Ella Sofia, was born on June 20, 2007.

Experiences a Resurgence

Following Gordon's disappointing performances in 2005 and 2006, some people within NASCAR began to wonder whether the four-time champion still had what it took to compete for another title. But Gordon's resurgence during the 2007 season seemed to

Jimmie Johnson's No. 48 car races ahead of Gordon's No. 24 car at the Ford 400 at Homestead-Miami Speedway in November 2007. Johnson also edged out Gordon for the Nextel Cup championship.

put that question to rest. He won six races that year, including one at Phoenix International Raceway in Arizona that marked the seventy-sixth victory of his career, tying Dale Earnhardt Sr. for seventh place on NASCAR's all-time list. He also showed remarkable consistency by posting thirty Top 10 finishes out of thirty-six events—six more than anyone else that year, and a new NASCAR record. It was undoubtedly one of the best season-long performances of his career.

People close to Gordon attributed his newfound success to the happiness and contentment he had achieved in his personal life. "I explain it like this," Bickford says. "If you get up in the morning and you're already not happy, you're not going to do your best work. But if life is perfect and everything is going your way, then you're going to do your job well, which for Jeff is to drive a car and communicate with his team. Jeff's now as happy as ever, both at the track and away from the track."[47] Gordon acknowledged that family life had a positive impact on his attitude and performance. "I'm in the best place in my life that I've ever been," he said. "That definitely plays a role in how you perform as a race car driver. I'm so happy to have Steve as my crew chief, and things couldn't be any better with Ingrid. Hopefully we can continue to roll."[48]

Gordon entered the 2007 Chase for the Cup in second place in the point standings. Following back-to-back victories at Talladega Superspeedway in Alabama and Charlotte Motor Speedway in North Carolina, he opened up a 68-point lead with five races left. Unfortunately for Gordon, his teammate Jimmie Johnson went on an amazing roll and won four of those five races. Johnson edged Gordon by 77 points to claim his second consecutive Nextel Cup championship. Gordon's disappointment was compounded by the fact that he had posted such a terrific season, finishing higher than Johnson in twenty-two of the thirty-six events. "I'm not getting any younger," he declared afterward. "I put up about as good a numbers as I know how to put up, and it wasn't enough. And that's tough to handle for a competitor."[49]

Takes a Backseat to Johnson

The 2008 season featured significant changes for both NASCAR and Hendrick Motorsports. NASCAR's premier race series underwent yet another change in sponsorship and became the Sprint Cup. NASCAR also introduced a new car design for the Sprint Cup Series called the Car of Tomorrow. Bigger and heavier than the older models, the redesigned cars were intended to improve driver safety. But many drivers, including Gordon, found the new cars to be bulky, sluggish, and difficult to handle. In the meantime, Hendrick Motorsports added a prominent new name to its stable of talented drivers. Dale Earnhardt Jr.—the son of Gordon's early rival and a hugely popular NASCAR driver in his own right—surprised many people by leaving the Dale Earnhardt Enterprises team for Hendrick. He took over the No. 5 car, which had been campaigned the previous year by Kyle Busch, and changed its number to 88.

Team owner Rick Hendrick, center, presents the Hendrick Motorsports lineup of drivers for the 2008 season, from left, Casey Mears, Jimmie Johnson, Dale Earnhardt Jr., and Gordon.

Despite the addition of Earnhardt Jr., Johnson solidified his position as the top driver on the Hendrick Motorsports team during the 2008 season. He achieved seven victories, including three during the Chase for the Cup, to join the legendary Cale Yarborough as the only drivers in NASCAR history to win three cup championships in a row. In the meantime, Gordon endured a tough season full of accidents and mechanical failures and failed to win a race. His nineteen Top 10 finishes allowed him to squeak into the Chase in tenth place, and he ended up finishing a disappointing seventh in the final point standings. Still, he was gracious in defeat and expressed nothing but friendship and support for Johnson. "I don't think many people could handle that situation better than he and I do," Gordon acknowledged. "I am happy for him, he's happy for me, but we also know how bad we want it for ourselves and our teams."[50]

Jimmie Johnson

Jimmie Johnson was born on September 17, 1975, in El Cajon, California, a suburb of San Diego. He grew up racing dirt bikes and dune buggies, and he earned several off-road racing championships during his teen years. In 1996, at the age of twenty-one, Johnson moved to Charlotte, North Carolina, hoping to compete in NASCAR.

After establishing himself as a promising short-course racer in the late 1990s, Johnson moved up to compete full time in the Nationwide Series in 2000. The following year, after learning that he was about to lose his sponsor, Johnson approached fellow California native Jeff Gordon for advice. As it turned out, Gordon needed a driver for a new cup series team. As co-owner of the car, Gordon decided to hire the relatively unknown Johnson to drive it.

In the decade that followed, Johnson dominated NASCAR like no other driver in history. He won 53 races in 327 starts, claimed an unprecedented five straight cup titles, and earned nearly $60 million in prize money. At the conclusion of the 2010 season, Johnson was named NASCAR's Driver of the Decade for the 2000s.

Johnson was so successful that Gordon often found himself in the unlikely position of studying his teammate's car and driving style for clues about how to improve his own performance. "I'm not ashamed to say I've learned from Jimmie," he admitted. "My ego's not so big where I'm afraid to borrow from his team."[51] Even though the No. 24 and No. 48 teams worked cooperatively and shared data, Gordon found that having inside information about the setup (allowable technical adjustments to chassis and suspension) of Johnson's car did not necessarily improve his own results. "Every time he's blistering fast, I say, 'Put that setup in,' and then I'm absolutely terrible," he noted. "I know what's under their car, and I always shake my head. I don't know how they make that work. But Jimmie's driving style is different enough that it does."[52]

Focuses on Winning

Prior to the start of the 2009 season, Gordon and Letarte decided to completely retool the 24 car. "We were sick of getting our butts kicked," Letarte explained. "So we tore everything down in the setup and started over."[53] Instead of basing their setup on what worked for Johnson, they adopted a new approach and built the car specifically to match Gordon's unique preferences. "Jimmie had been running good for so long that we just tried to emulate what he was doing," Gordon acknowledged. "But that just didn't work. Jimmie and I have different driving styles. I don't use as much brake getting into the corner as he does. And I never felt comfortable in the car. I couldn't push it to the limit because I was loose into the corner."[54] The changes eliminated this problem and gave Gordon greater confidence than he had felt since the Car of Tomorrow was introduced.

Gordon and crew chief Steve Letarte, right, review the results of a testing session in 2008. The pair decided to retool the No. 24 car to be more competitive the following season.

Gordon also worked hard to improve his physical fitness during the off-season. He launched a new workout routine that involved a great deal of stretching. The workouts helped eliminate some nagging back problems and put him into the best shape of his life. All the hard work paid off as he won a race in April and sat atop the point standings in the early part of the 2009 season. "This is the best my body has felt and the best my cars have felt in a long time," Gordon declared in 2009. "I feel like we can win every week, which is something I didn't think last year."[55] Unfortunately for Gordon, he performed less consistently as the year wore on. Although he ended the season with a series-leading twenty-five Top 10 finishes, Gordon wound up third in the point standings. In the meantime, his teammate Jimmie Johnson became the first driver in NASCAR history to win four cup championships in a row.

Gordon entered his eighteenth cup season in 2010 having won only one race in the previous two years. Determined to return to his winning ways, he adopted an intensely focused and fiercely competitive new attitude. On a couple of occasions during the 2010 season, Gordon uncharacteristically clashed with other drivers, including his teammates. When Johnson made a mental error that caused Gordon to crash during a race at Talladega

Gordon's crashed car sits on the track at Texas Motor Speedway after getting bumped into the wall by Jeff Burton while the race was under the caution flag. An enraged Gordon lept from his car to fight with Burton on the side of the track.

Superspeedway, for instance, Gordon let his anger show. "The 48 is testing my patience, I can tell you that," he said afterward. "It takes a lot to make me mad and I am pissed. I don't know what it is with me and him right now."[56] In a November race at Texas Motor Speedway in Texas, fellow driver Jeff Burton tapped Gordon's car during a caution lap (a period when competitors are required to slow down and maintain their positions due to unsafe conditions on the track), causing him to crash into the wall. Gordon reacted by jumping out of his car, stomping across the track, and engaging in a shoving match with Burton. Some observers attributed Gordon's actions to frustration with his own performance, but others claimed that he was simply expressing his passionate desire to win.

Gordon ended up with a respectable twenty-five Top 10 finishes in 2010, but he never managed to break through for a victory all season. "It's not from lack of being competitive," says team owner Rick Hendrick. "We've led a lot of races, we've been up front, just for whatever reason, we've been a little snakebit."[57] Despite looking strong in the early part of the season, Gordon faltered in the Chase for the Cup once again. He ended up ninth in the point standings—his lowest finish since 2005—while his friend, teammate, and former protégé Johnson claimed his record fifth consecutive Sprint Cup title. Although Gordon was pleased to share in the championship as part owner of the 48 car, he remained determined to earn his own fifth title as a driver. "What I am really focused on is, what do we got to do to be better next year?"[58] he stated.

Continues the Quest for a Fifth Championship

By the end of the 2010 season, it was clear that Gordon—at thirty-nine years old—was no longer the dominant force that he had been in his prime. After he ended the year mired in a sixty-one-race winless streak—the longest of his career—NASCAR fans and analysts alike speculated about the source of the problem. Some people blamed his car, saying that it was not fast enough

Gordon's No. 24 car displays a new paint scheme before the start of the 2011 season, emphasizing his sponsorship deal with AARP's Drive to End Hunger campaign.

and suggesting that Hendrick Motorsports devoted a larger share of its resources to Johnson's team. Others claimed that Gordon's driving ability had declined over the years. Finally, some people questioned whether Gordon still possessed the same will to win that he had as a younger driver. After all, Gordon had surpassed $100 million in career earnings and settled into a comfortable life as a husband and father. His wife gave birth to their second child, son Leo Benjamin, on August 9, 2010.

But people who knew Gordon argued that he was still a fierce competitor—perhaps even more so than earlier in his career, since his lack of recent success had given him something to prove. "I've seen a fire in his eyes that I haven't seen since he started. I mean, a bunch of people say he's like he used to be. I say that he's more than he used to be. He's more determined. He's driving harder," said team owner Rick Hendrick. "He's a competitor. You see Jimmie and the success he's had, whereas Jeff's been competitive but hasn't won as much. Well, he's saying, 'I'm going to show the world that they maybe think I'm all done, but I'm a long ways from being done.'"[59]

Some motor-sports experts argued that the problem was not that Gordon had become weaker but rather that the overall level of NASCAR competition had grown stronger. "Gordon is still

NASCAR Sponsors

NASCAR racing is very expensive. Building a single race car costs more than $150,000, and most teams go through between fifteen and eighteen cars per season. Adding in the costs of fuel, tires, salaries for the driver and pit crew, transportation for the team and equipment, and other expenses, a typical NASCAR team spends more than $20 million per year.

To help pay the high costs of racing, virtually everything involved with NASCAR has a corporate sponsor, including cars, tracks, events, and even entire race series. Corporate sponsorship of NASCAR originated in 1972, when the R.J. Reynolds tobacco company

Gordon's race suit features the logos of multiple sponsors. Companies invest millions of dollars to associate their products and services with high-profile racers and their cars.

purchased the right to sponsor stock-car racing's premier series and named it the Winston Cup. In 2004 the telephone company Nextel/Sprint paid $700 million to take over primary sponsorship of the series for ten years and it became the Sprint Cup.

Big businesses—from candy and cereal manufacturers to retail stores and websites—pay between $15 million and $20 million to be the primary sponsor of a Sprint Cup car for an entire season. Primary sponsorship enables the company to choose the car's paint scheme, display its logo prominently on the hood, and use the likeness of both car and driver in its advertising. A partial sponsorship with a smaller logo might cost $1.5 million per season. In return for their investment, sponsors get their brand names exposed to millions of race fans who tend buy products associated with NASCAR in general and their favorite drivers in particular.

very hungry to win," wrote *Yahoo! Sports* auto-racing analyst Jay Hart. "And though he hasn't been to victory lane in more than a year, he's still very, very competitive.... Comparing Gordon to everyone else, he's still very much a top-five driver. It's only when you compare him to Jeff Gordon circa 1998 that the chinks in the armor appear."[60] Other racing insiders noted that—with the startling exception of Jimmie Johnson—few people in NASCAR history managed to remain on top year after year. "It is so difficult to stay at that level," said two-time cup champion Terry Labonte. "You don't see anybody who's ever been able to do that. It's not just one guy or one person. It's tougher for a whole team to stay there and keep doing that. You have 40 other teams shooting at you all the time."[61]

Gordon agrees that the greater equality among teams made winning a championship more challenging during the second decade of his career. "Because the sport has changed, competition is not only stronger but it's deeper throughout the field than it's ever been," he acknowledges. "It's harder to win."[62] Despite the tougher competitive atmosphere, though, Gordon plans to keep trying for that fifth title for at least a few more years. "Five years ago, I thought 2010 might be my last year. I was having some issues with my back and I just thought maybe I would be ready to step away," he admits. "But I'm not. I'm so passionate about it. I am still competitive and my health, from my back standpoint, has gotten better and that's giving me years to be behind the wheel."[63]

In late 2010 Gordon announced a new, three-year sponsorship deal with AARP Foundation's Drive to End Hunger campaign. It was the first cause-related primary sponsorship in NASCAR history. Gordon was excited about the opportunity to help raise awareness of the problem of hunger among older Americans. "It just amazes me—millions of Americans are forced to make a choice between going hungry and medicine," he explains. "And 6 million of those are 60 or over."[64] Gordon also learned that he would get a new crew chief for the 2011 season. Hendrick Motorsports announced that Alan Gustafson would switch from Mark Martin's No. 5 car to Gordon's 24, while Steve Letarte would move to the 88 team and work with Dale Earnhardt Jr. Many observers felt that Gustafson—widely respected as a technical wizard—could help Gordon return to the top of the standings. "The performance for Gordon is about to go way up," wrote Terry Blount of ESPN. "Gustafson, possibly the second-most talented crew chief in Sprint Cup behind only five-time champ Chad Knaus [of Johnson's 48 team], is exactly what Gordon needs for a shot at title No. 5."[65]

Introduction: Changing the Face of NASCAR

1. Jeff MacGregor. "Speed Demon: Jeff Gordon Is Deified by Millions as the Paragon of All That's Right About America, and Vilified by Millions More as the Blue-Eyed Devil Who Will Be the Wrack and Ruin of NASCAR. Could They Both Be Right?" *Sports Illustrated*, February 10, 2003, p. 68.
2. Jeff Gordon. *Jeff Gordon: Racing Back to the Front—My Memoir*. With Steve Eubanks. New York: Atria, 2003, p. 221.

Chapter 1: Racing Through Childhood

3. Gordon. *Jeff Gordon*, p. 20.
4. Quoted in MacGregor. "Speed Demon," p. 68.
5. Quoted in Dan Kelly. "Fast Company: Check Out How Jeff Gordon Raced to the Pinnacle of NASCAR Success--If You Think You Can Keep Up!" *Boys' Life*, August 2005, p. 40.
6. MacGregor. "Speed Demon," p. 68.
7. Gordon. *Jeff Gordon*, p. 30.
8. Quoted in "Biographical Information." Jeff Gordon Online. http://gordonline.com/bio.html.
9. Gordon. *Jeff Gordon*, p. 38.
10. Quoted in Jerry Adler. "Chariots of Fire." *Newsweek*, July 28, 1997, p. 54.
11. Quoted in Ryan McGee. "Jeff Gordon: Entrepreneur, Employee, Spokesman, Humanitarian, Everyman." *ESPN the Magazine*, September 16, 2007. http://sports.espn.go.com/rpm/news/story?series=2&id=3022895.
12. Gordon. *Jeff Gordon*, p. 43.

Chapter 2: Breaking into NASCAR

13. Quoted in MacGregor. "Speed Demon," p. 68.
14. Quoted in McGee. "Jeff Gordon: Entrepreneur, Employee, Spokesman, Humanitarian, Everyman."
15. Quoted in Gordon. *Jeff Gordon*, p. 47.
16. Gordon. *Jeff Gordon*, p. 78.
17. Gordon. *Jeff Gordon*, p. 84.

Chapter 3: Becoming a Champion

18. Gordon. *Jeff Gordon*, p. 94.
19. Gordon. *Jeff Gordon*, p. 95.
20. Gordon. *Jeff Gordon*, p. 103.
21. Roland Lazenby. "Dominators of Sport: 1997." *Sport*, January 1998, p. 55.
22. Quoted in Mike Puma. "Gordon, a Boy and His Car." ESPNcom. http://espn.go.com/classic/biography/s/Gordon _Jeff.html.
23. Jerry Adler. "Chariots of Fire." *Newsweek*, July 28, 1997, p. 54.
24. Gordon. *Jeff Gordon*, p. 95.
25. Quoted in Ed Hinton. "Formula for a Championship: Jeff Gordon and Crew Chief Ray Evernham Have Winning Down to a Science, and the Secret Lies in Their Personal Chemistry." *Sports Illustrated*, November 25, 1998, p. 14.

Chapter 4: Winning with a New Team

26. Quoted in Hinton. "Formula for a Championship," p. 14.
27. Gordon. *Jeff Gordon*, p. 124.
28. Lars Anderson. "Comeback Kid: With His New Crew, Jeff Gordon Was Back on Top, Answering All Doubters by Winning His Fourth Points Title—This One Especially Sweet." *Sports Illustrated*, December 3, 2001, p. 16.
29. Quoted in Hinton. "Formula for a Championship," p. 14.
30. Gordon. *Jeff Gordon*, p. 160.
31. Quoted in Anderson. "Comeback Kid," p. 16.

32. Gordon. *Jeff Gordon*, p. 187.
33. Gordon. *Jeff Gordon*, p. xix.
34. Gordon. *Jeff Gordon*, p. xii.
35. Quoted in Ken Willis. "Gordon: Leader of the Pack: Now More Comfortable Taking a Dominant Role with His Team, Jeff Gordon Is Back on Pace to Becoming the Greatest Stock Car Driver of All Time." *Auto Racing Digest*, February/March 2002, p. 54.

Chapter 5: Maturing as a Driver and Team Owner

36. Quoted in Mark Bechtel. "New Kid on the Block: Jimmie Johnson Thought He Might Learn a Thing or Two from His Mentor, Jeff Gordon. Turned Out the Kid Picked Up a Little Wisdom from his Protégé," *Sports Illustrated*, December 1, 2002, p. 70.
37. Quoted in Bechtel. "New Kid on the Block," p. 70.
38. Quoted in Bechtel. "New Kid on the Block," p. 70.
39. Gordon. *Jeff Gordon*, p. 112.
40. Quoted in Larry Woody. "From Choirboy to Playboy: Footloose and Fancy-Free, Jeff Gordon Is Eschewing His Squeaky-Clean Image and Coming out of His Cocoon." *Auto Racing Digest*, December 2003, p. 34.
41. Quoted in Mark McCarter. "A Question of Standards: Jeff Gordon Is Off the Championship Pace for the Second Straight Season. Call It a Slump—But Only Because So Much More Is Expected of Him." *Sporting News*, October 6, 2003, p. 26.
42. Quoted in Woody. "From Choirboy to Playboy," p. 34.
43. Quoted in Matt Crossman. "Back on Track: Jeff Gordon's Thrilling Win at Daytona—the Product of Laser-Sharp Concentration and Dazzling Skill—Is Proof NASCAR's Focus, Thankfully, Again Is on the Drivers." *Sporting News*, March 4, 2005, p. 12.
44. Quoted in Matt Crossman. "Avoid at the Top: Four-Time Champion Failed to Make the Chase for the NASCAR Nextel Cup for One Simple Reason: He Can't Count on His Cars." *Sporting News*, September 23, 2005, p. 30.

45. Quoted in Lars Anderson. "Here Comes Mr. Gordon." *Sports Illustrated*, July 2, 2007, p. 64.

46. Quoted in Anderson. "Here Comes Mr. Gordon," p. 64.

47. Quoted in Anderson. "Here Comes Mr. Gordon," p. 64.

48. Quoted in Anderson. "Here Comes Mr. Gordon," p. 64.

49. Quoted in Tom McCarthy. "Gordon's 2007 Sets New Standard of Measurement." NASCAR.com, November 19, 2007. www.nascar.com/2007/news/opinion/11/19/jgordon.runner.up.standard/index.html.

50. Quoted in Jenna Fryer. "Friendship Intact as Hendrick Teammates Jeff Gordon, Jimmie Johnson Vie for Title." *USA Today*, November 10, 2007. http://www.usatoday.com/sports/motor/2007-11-10-3517089944_x.htm.

51. Quoted in Bechtel. "New Kid on the Block," p. 70.

52. Quoted in "Jimmie Johnson." *Biography Today*. Edited by Cherie D. Abbey. Detroit, MI: Omnigraphics, 2009.

53. Quoted in Lars Anderson. "Wake-up Call." *Sports Illustrated*, March 16, 2009, p. 66.

54. Quoted in Anderson. "Here Comes Mr. Gordon," p. 64.

55. Quoted in Anderson. "Here Comes Mr. Gordon," p. 66.

56. Quoted in Tom Jensen. "Meet the New Jeff Gordon (Hint: It's the Old Jeff Gordon)." *Racer*, July 2010, p. 44.

57. Quoted in "Limping to Finish, Gordon Focuses on the Future." *New York Times*, October 30, 2010. www.nytimes.com/2010/10/31/sports/autoracing/31nascar.html.

58. Quoted in "Limping to Finish."

59. Quoted in Jensen. "Meet the New Jeff Gordon," p. 44.

60. Jay Hart. "Beginning of the End for Gordon? Not Yet." Yahoo! Sports, November 9, 2010. http://sports.yahoo.com/nascar/news?slug=jh-happyhour110910.

61. Quoted in McCarter. "A Question of Standards," p. 26.

62. Quoted in McCarter. "A Question of Standards," p. 26.

63. Quoted in "Limping to Finish."

64. Quoted in Jack Curry. "Racing to Beat Hunger: Why NASCAR Champ Jeff Gordon Is Teaming Up with AARP." AARP, October 2010. www.aarp.org/giving-back/charitable -giving/info-10-2010/jeff_gordon_aarp_drive_to_end _hunger.html.

65. Terry Blount. "Jeff Gordon the Big Winner in Shake-up." ESPN.com, November 24, 2010. http://sports.espn.go.com/ rpm/nascar/cup/columns/story?columnist=blount_terry&id =5846436&campaign=rss&source=RPMHeadlines.

1971

Jeffrey Michael Gordon is born on August 4 in Vallejo, California.

1991

Gordon makes his debut in NASCAR's Busch Series (later known as the Nationwide Series) and earns Rookie of the Year honors.

1993

Gordon completes his first full season in NASCAR's Winston Cup Series (later known as the Sprint Cup Series) and is named Rookie of the Year.

1994

On May 29, Gordon claims his first Winston Cup victory in the Coca-Cola 600 at Charlotte Motor Speedway in North Carolina. On November 26, Gordon marries former Miss Winston, Brooke Sealey.

1995

Gordon wins the Winston Cup championship in his third full season competing on the circuit. At twenty-four, he becomes the youngest champion in modern NASCAR history.

1997

Gordon wins ten races—including the prestigious Daytona 500—and achieves his second Winston Cup championship.

1998

In one of the most dominant season-long performances in NASCAR history, Gordon wins thirteen races and posts an incredible twenty-six Top 5 finishes to capture his third Winston Cup title.

2001

Gordon becomes the third driver in NASCAR history to win four Winston Cup championships.

2002

Hendrick Motorsports launches a fourth race team. As part owner of the new 48 car, Gordon hires Jimmie Johnson to drive it.

2006

Three years after finalizing his divorce from his first wife, Gordon marries Belgian model Ingrid Vandebosch on November 6.

2007

Gordon's daughter Ella Sofia is born on June 20.

2010

Gordon's son Leo Benjamin is born on August 9.

2011

Gordon enters his nineteenth cup season with a new sponsor, AARP Foundation's Drive to End Hunger campaign, and a new crew chief, Alan Gustafson.

Books

Jim Gigliotti. *Jeff Gordon: Simply the Best*. Chanhassen, MN: Tradition, 2003. This readable juvenile biography from the World of NASCAR series covers Gordon's early life and racing career.

Marty Gitlin. *Jeff Gordon: Racing's Brightest Star*. Berkeley Heights, NJ: Enslow, 2008. This detailed juvenile biography traces Gordon's development as a young driver and his emergence as a dominant force in NASCAR.

Jeff Gordon. *Jeff Gordon: Racing Back to the Front—My Memoir*. With Steve Eubanks. New York: Atria, 2003. Published after Gordon's fourth Winston Cup championship, this book offers first-person recollections of Gordon's childhood and experiences in NASCAR.

J. Poolos. *Jeff Gordon: NASCAR Driver*. New York: Rosen, 2007. Part of the Behind the Wheel series of driver biographies, this readable book chronicles Gordon's racing career and personal life.

Internet Sources

Mike Puma. "Gordon, a Boy and His Car." ESPN.com, October 2005. http://espn.go.com/classic/biography/s/Gordon_Jeff.html. This online article provides a retrospective of Gordon's racing career and describes his impact on the world of NASCAR.

Periodicals

Jerry Adler. "Chariots of Fire." *Newsweek*, July 28, 1997. This article follows Gordon's rise to stardom and examines the sources of his extreme popularity—and extreme unpopularity—among NASCAR fans.

Lars Anderson. "Here Comes Mr. Gordon." *Sports Illustrated*, July 2, 2007. Published six years after Gordon won his fourth

Winston Cup title, this article analyzes the state of Gordon's racing career and identifies factors that could contribute to his future success.

Websites

Hendrick Motorsports (www.hendrickmotorsports.com). The official website of Hendrick Motorsports provides a time line of Gordon's racing career, a photo gallery, and news and information about the 24 team.

Jeff Gordon (www.jeffgordon.com). Gordon's official website features up-to-date news and information, biographies of the driver and his crew, and a personal photo gallery and blog.

NASCAR (www.nascar.com). NASCAR's website offers an official driver's page for Gordon that includes a biography, news articles, and season and career statistics.

Picture Credits

Cover Photo: © Sean Michaels/Retna/Retna Ltd./Corbis
AP Images/PR Newswire, 77
AP Images/Bruce Chapman, 44
AP Images/Chris O'Meara, 53
AP Images/Chuck Burton, 72, 74
AP Images/Dave Martin, 33
AP Images/Dima Gavrysh, 69
AP Images/Gene Blythe, 39
AP Images/LM Otero, 75
AP Images/Mike McCarn, 12
AP Images/Robert E. Klein, 29
AP Images/Steve Helber, 25
AP Images/Ric Feld, 41, 55
AP Images/Wilfredo Lee, 58
Brian E. Cleary/Getty Images Sport/Getty Images, 42
Chris Graythen/Getty Images Sport/Getty Images, 40, 70, 78
Craig Jones/Getty Images Sport/Getty Images, 48
Doug Benc/Getty Images Sport/Getty Images, 9, 66
Eliot J. Schechter/Getty Images Sport/ Getty Images, 60
Elsa/Getty Images Sport/Getty Images, 62
Focus On Sport/Getty Images Sport/Getty Images, 31
Jamie Squire/Getty Images Sport/Getty Images, 65
© Pete Klinger/Alamy, 19
RacingOne/ISC Archives/Getty Images, 14, 15, 22, 27, 36, 50
Ron Hoskins/Getty Images Sport/Getty Images, 17
© Sam Sharpe/The Sharpe Image/Corbis, 52

Laurie Collier Hillstrom has written and edited award-winning reference works on a wide range of subjects, including American history, biography, popular culture, and international environmental issues. She is the author of several previous volumes in the People in the News series, including *Al Gore*, *Robert Downey Jr.*, and *Dale Earnhardt Jr.* She lives in Michigan with her husband, Kevin Hillstrom, and twin daughters, Allison and Lindsay.